M

A Life from Beginning to End

Table of Contents

Introduction

Born the day after Christmas on December 26, 1893, to a wealthy farmer named Mao Yichang, and his wife Wen Qimei, Mao Zedong began life under the auspices of a wealthy aristocratic family in China's Hunan Province. By all accounts, despite being born into what would have been easily termed a life of luxury by his peers, due to the severe disciplinary measures of his father, Mao's upbringing was rather harsh.

Almost as soon as Mao could walk his father made him work, and by the time Mao was six years old he was already working as a full-time farm hand for his father. In addition to this manual labor, Mao was enrolled into primary school starting at the age of eight while he continued to toil on the farm in the early morning and late into the evening.

His father, who was born a peasant and had risen through the ranks, did not have much of an opportunity for education himself but made sure that Mao received his. As Mao proved to be a particularly bright student, Mao's father saw yet another opportunity for his son to help out with the family business by putting him in charge of the family's financial accounts.

Before he was even a teenager, the industrious Mao Zedong was working as a toughened farm hand and a wizardly accountant. Mao was the oldest surviving son in his family, and as such, much was placed on his young shoulders. It was also during this period of bailing hay and keeping track of his father's books that Mao first developed much of his political outlook on the world.

And as the young Mao's ideologies continued to ferment, events in the neighboring capital of Hunan,

Changsha, would soon bring these views right to his own doorstep. The famine, eventually reaching right into Mao's neighborhood, became so bad that local peasants began to steal his father's own supply of grain.

Although Mao understood and sympathized with the plight of his neighbors who were stealing from his father, he did not approve of their methodology. The starving peasants felt that they had no choice, and growing increasingly militant, developed the slogan, "Eat Rice without Charge." Mao couldn't fathom why his countrymen were in such a poor state.

He still couldn't bring himself to condone the seizure of him and his father's hard-earned commodities. What Mao could fathom even less was how the duplicitous government of China could promise rioters and grain stealers forgiveness of their discord if they simply desist, and then once they do so, immediately cut off the relenting rioters' heads.

It was in this corrupt environment in September of 1909 that Mao entered the East Mountain Higher Primary School in the city of Xiangxiang. This primary school followed the example of and was modeled after, the private schools of the time that were run by foreign missionaries. As much as Mao was eager to learn, he was almost immediately singled out by his peers at the school as an outsider.

Picked on by the city dwellers for his thick rural accent, and also ridiculed for—of all things—his height, Mao was often ostracized by his fellow students. Mao Zedong was also a few years older than his classmates at the time of his enrollment, which was yet another source of derision, yet despite these obstacles, Mao was determined to succeed.

Of particular interest for Mao during his coursework at East Mountain was his study of world history. He loved to read about the rise of nations and powerful leaders such as Napoleon Bonaparte and George Washington. It was through these two revolutionary figures that Mao began first to grasp the concept of a future revolution in China.

Zedong would stay on at East Mountain Primary school for just two years, from September 1909 to September 1911, before moving on to a secondary school in the capital of Changsha. He would only spend about four weeks at this school before this avid history buff would be caught up in some pretty major events in history himself.

Chapter One

Where Revolution Was Made

"A revolution is an insurrection, an act of violence by which one class overthrows another."

—Mao Zedong

The world of Chinese politics was rife with intrigue when an 18-year-old Mao Zedong arrived by riverboat steamer to the city of Changsha. At this point in his young life, for the rural-born Mao Zedong, Changsha was the biggest city he had ever seen. Although he was enthusiastic for the setting, Mao would only remain enrolled in school at Changsha for four weeks.

Shortly after his arrival, Mao, like many of his fellow students, had been inspired by the nationalist movement of Sun Yat-sen. Riding on this tidal wave of national enthusiasm, Mao dropped out of school and enlisted in the Hunan revolutionary army. During his service Mao did not see much fighting; most of his tasks involved running letters and doing other menial errands for his superior officers.

By 1912 the conflict had concluded itself with the proclamation of the "Republic of China" and the official abdication of the last Quin Emperor from the throne. During all of these monumental events in Chinese history, Mao Zedong was just 19 years old and found himself drifting listlessly through the city streets of Changsha without any direction.

In a quick succession of time, he tried many things. He enrolled in a Police Academy, attempted Law School, and even tried his hand as a soap maker, but each and every time he somehow fell short of anything substantial. Unsure of what to do, and what institution to attend, Mao decided to teach himself. He rented out a bed in a local boarding house, and when he wasn't sleeping, he was at the local library poring over books of history and philosophy.

Mao relished his learning even when it was self-taught, but that bed back at the boarding house cost money, and Mao soon found himself running out of it. His father had been supplementing his income with a modest allowance, but, disappointed in what he viewed as "aimless drifting," Mao Zedong's father stopped sending him money. Desperate for answers and a purpose in life Mao finally settled on a vocation and enrolled in the "Fourth Normal School of Changsha" in the fall of 1913.

It was at this school that Mao Zedong would meet one of the most pivotal figures in his life, a social science teacher by the name of Yang Changji. It was under the tutelage of Yang that Mao was directed to channel some of the finer points of his political ideology. It was Yang who encouraged Mao to take his theory into practice, which Mao did by joining several revolutionary student organizations.

Mao would graduate from the Fourth Normal School five years later in 1918. Just months after his graduation, however, tragedy would strike in the form of his mother's passing. After the death of his mother, Mao felt that the last tie that connected him to the family farm had been severed, and soon followed after Professor Yang to the Chinese capital of Beijing.

Here on his meager budget, the best lodging that he could come by was one room in a boarding house that he had to share with seven other men. As unbelievable as it may sound, these roommates supposedly even shared the same bed! Mao would later recount that all seven of them shared one large "kang," a type of heated bed used in the colder regions of China.

According to Mao, conditions were so cramped that he couldn't even turn over in bed without knocking his roommates, sleeping next to him, off the bed. Whether there is some exaggeration on Mao Zedong's part remains to be seen, but he must have been threadbare regardless. Things only began to look up for him when Professor Yang managed to get him a job at the Beijing University's library.

Even though Mao never officially enrolled at the university, due to his status as an employee he was granted special permission to attend many of the lectures on campus. It was here that he was first introduced to the concepts of Karl Marx. It was also here that Mao Zedong was first introduced to love in the form of Yang's daughter, Yang Kaihui.

The two developed a relationship after Mao began staying over in Yang's house. Shortly after her father's death in January of 1920, Yang Kaihui would end up marrying her father's star pupil: Mao Zedong.

Just previous to their marriage, Mao had been appointed headmaster of a junior section of the First Normal School, which put him in a prime position to shape his own political destiny, as he began the first "Marxist Society" of Changsha. It was here, in this nondescript school in 1920's China, where Mao Zedong's revolution was made.

Chapter Two

Mao Comes Into His Own

"Learn from the masses, and then teach them."

—Mao Zedong

During the early 1920's Mao Zedong saw his family expand as he had his first son with Kaihui, a baby boy by the name of Anying in 1921, and another son named Anqing in 1923. It was in July of 1921 that China witnessed a birth of another kind when a group of Russian advisors from the newly founded Soviet Union paid a visit to Shanghai.

Here, these international communist agents, with the aid of local Chinese Marxists, sought to create an official communist party in China. Mao Zedong just happened to be one of these local Chinese Marxists who were called upon for this establishment, and henceforth has been known as one of the early founders of the Chinese communist system.

Obtaining the rank of Chairman for all of Hunan Province, Mao immediately sought to make a name for himself while he eagerly tried to swell the ranks of the communist party. His first challenge, however, was to convince his communist counterparts and backers in Moscow that China's real proletariat wasn't in the factory but the fields.

His Russian colleagues tried to persuade him early on that the revolution needed to be taken to the Chinese cities, but Mao, a child of the rural provinces himself, saw things differently; he believed that the strong-willed peasants, who were much greater in number than any potential working class proletariat in the big cities, were the real force to be reckoned with in China.

Remembering the revolts that led to peasants rising up and stealing his father's grain, Mao knew that if he could only tap into the peasant farmer's discontent, he would have a huge army of followers at his beck and call. He continued to receive staunch resistance against this theory, however, and the other members of the communist party overruled his plans, insisting that revolution was to begin in the cities.

However, by the early 1920's, the fledgling communist party had more to worry about than these simple ideological squabbles. With various warring internal factions, coupled with increasing foreign encroachments from both the Western powers and the Empire of Japan, the political landscape of China seemed to be a mine field. The Communist Party of China (CCP) had a main antagonist in the form of the "Kuomintang," a Chinese nationalist group controlled by the decidedly anti-communist ranks of the landed aristocracy of China.

The two groups were always at odds, but in May of 1925 when its original leader Sun Yat-sen died and was succeeded by the leadership of Chiang Kai-shek. Kai-shek became determined to get rid of communism in China, but the threat of an aggressive, fascist and expansionist Japan would bring Chaing Kai-shek and the Kuomintang to temporarily forget their differences with the communists in order to address these more pressing external threats.

The first of these overtures happened when a group of officials from the Russian communist party brokered a truce with the two previously opposed sides. In exchange for Chaing Kai-shek's cooperation, he received much-needed military and financial aid from the Soviets. As a result, the Chinese Communists and the Kuomintang, as strange bedfellows as they may have been, became official allies.

Mao supported many of the early leaders of the Kuomintang Nationalists because he felt that they were instrumental in support of rural peasants against the local warlords and land owners that were oppressing them. Sure enough, as Chaing Kai-shek's army pushed through rural China and dethroned the warlord leaders, vast multitudes of peasant farmers rose up in their wake, much to the satisfaction of an observant Mao Zedong.

As Mao put it at the time, "Every bit of the dignity and prestige built up by the landlords is being swept up into the dust." While much of their destabilizing actions against the landed class of Chinese nobility was, in fact, a direct aid to communist sensibility, the Kuomintang themselves never imagined that their actions were helping to hand China over to communism.

By the late 1920's, however, in light of growing support for the CCP, the Chinese Nationalists began to grow more concerned. By 1927 they had turned on the communists, cutting official correspondence before turning their guns on the communist leadership themselves. The first site of this sudden onslaught of Nationalist aggression was in the city of Shanghai where 5000 CCP members were shot dead.

These attacks were then followed by mass executions in Beijing, Guangzhou, and even Mao's own home province of Hunan. As a result, many communists who found themselves under this incessant barrage of aggression from the Kuomintang were exiled or otherwise sent into hiding. However, the communists would soon rebound and begin reclaiming their own territory, starting with the recovery of Nanchang, a town just northeast of Changsa, which they successfully won back from the Nationalists on August 1st, 1927.

This win was short lived by the communists, however, and the Red Army was soon kicked right out of the city. The communists then turned their sights on the neighboring Changsa, with Mao himself ordered by the CCP central committee to lead four attacking regiments. As soon as Mao and his men arrived on the scene, however, it was clear that they were completely outmatched by their opposition.

Knowing that it would be a catastrophic loss to engage the superior force directly, Mao defied his directives and ordered his men to retreat back into the wilderness. They found refuge in the neighboring Chingkang Mountains, where they hid among the rocks and waited for their next move. Many men, being holed up in a desolate mountain wilderness with limited supplies and a massive army on their heels, would crack.

However, Mao simply refined his efforts, and even in the middle of the mountains, he made sure that his men were well-disciplined. Many of the locals soon took note of the strange sight of the mountain refugees; some even joined, greatly impressed by the communist guerrilla fighters eking out an existence right in their midst.

Among these new recruits, many deserters from the Nationalist army were also among those that swelled the ranks. It was here that Mao became a truly independent leader, and, holed up in his own sort of mountain kingdom with his own loyal followers, he began to become further and further from the grasp of even his own CCP Central Committee leaders; Mao Zedong came into his own.

Chapter Three

Mao, the Pragmatist

"Swollen in head, weak in legs, sharp in tongue but empty in belly."

—Mao Zedong

Due to Mao's persistent defiance of the CCP Central Committee's directives, Mao was actually briefly expelled from the party as punishment for what they viewed to be his rogue military actions. Even so, by 1928, the CCP was giving Mao Zedong marching orders once again, sending him out to Hunan province, where he was told to help foment communist revolution.

As soon as Mao and his men arrived on the scene, however, they were immediately engaged by a large Kuomintang contingent and were forced to make a protracted retreat. Even worse for Mao was the fact that while his small band of soldiers was being chased out of Hunan, his very mountain base of Chingkang was being overrun by nationalist troops.

All of Mao's army was scattered at this point, but as they wandered through the countryside, they managed to meet up with another CPC regiment led by Zhu De and Lin Biao, two senior commanders of the Red Army, and regroup. With their combined efforts, they began to take Chingkang back but could not hold on to their mountain base for very long and were quickly driven back in a massive Kuomintang counter attack.

In the weeks that followed, Mao's Red Army would fight a long and bloody guerrilla war to retake the mountain base once and for all. It was during this bloody period that Mao met the second love of his life, a young communist ideologue named He Zizhen. It didn't seem to bother either one of them that Mao already had a wife, and an intense affair soon bloomed between the two of them.

Once Mao and his loyal followers managed to retake their mountain base for good finally, Mao decided to expand his communist stronghold even further and pushed out his reach down from the mountains and into Jiangxi province. Here he established his first "Soviet," or Russian-styled self-governing communist community. In this communal dwelling, there would be no private ownership of property, and all land was seized from landowners and turned over to the peasants to work as farm collectives.

These measures actually did improve the lives of many of the poor people in rural China, but this newfound prosperity of the peasants also brought persecution and outright imprisonment to the landowners whose property was confiscated. For Mao, such drastic, socially engineered reversals of fortune were just what the doctor had ordered. It was only the CCP that came to question who was writing out the prescription.

When CCP party bosses from Shanghai arrived on the scene in Jiangxi, as soon as his rival communists arrived, they immediately connived to limit the scope of power that the once unquestioned authority that Mao had in the region. Primary among these measures was the stripping of most of Mao's leadership power in favor of an up-and-coming communist party member named Zhou Enlai.

With Zhou Enlai in charge of the Red Army of Jiangxi, Mao's role was reduced to as hardly even be mentionable. As his relationship with the CCP deteriorated even further, he was even temporarily placed under house arrest. As Mao

Zedong's political fortunes deteriorated, so did his health. Mao began to be plagued by bouts of malaria and other common pestilences of the humid subtropical climate of the region.

It was while Mao was recovering from his latest round of malaria that he heard the news of his sister's death at the hands of Chiang Kai-shek's army in August of 1929. This sad news would be followed a year in October of 1930 by even worse tidings from Mao's personal family in Changsha when his own wife Yang Kaihui was detained by the Kuomintang, brutally interrogated, and shot dead when she refused to reveal her husband's whereabouts.

It is hard to say how much the tidings of his wife's tragic end affected Mao, but as soon as he heard the news of his wife's death, he wasted no time in marrying his mistress, his longtime companion in the mountains, He Zhizhen. In love and in war, Mao was ever the pragmatist.

Chapter Four

The Gift of Unity

"A revolution is an insurrection, an act of violence by which one class overthrows another."

—Mao Zedong

In the aftermath of so much personal trauma and duress suffered by the Kuomintang Nationalists, and to some extent even his own communist party members, strangely enough, when Mao Zedong heard tidings of the 1931 Japanese invasion of Manchuria, it almost came as a relief. Due to the imminent outside threat, both his rivals in the communist party and the Kuomintang Nationalists that were previously holding Mao in a vice-like grip had to release their hold in order to focus on the Japanese threat.

Shortly after Mao received this relief, he was finally given the go-ahead for a long-desired project, a "land verification" effort in which he sought to redistribute the land further and create even more collective farms in his local "Soviet" commune in Jiangxi. It was during this period that Mao also took the opportunity to expand his family, having two children virtually back to back with his new wife, He Zhizhen.

Whereas their first child was sent to a nanny in rural China and died in infancy, for this second child, named Anhong, Mao was determined to keep this baby by his side. For the first few months of baby Anhong's infancy, Mao and He Zhizhen lived in a remote, hillside temple, in almost complete isolation.

Thanks to the brazen Japanese attack on Shanghai in 1932, everyone in China, whether they had Nationalist or Communist leanings, were placing all of their efforts in the cause of expelling the foreign invaders. Most crucial in this were the Chinese outposts in Inner Mongolia near the Japanese-installed puppet state of Manchukuo in Manchuria.

Japan soon began pushing from Inner Mongolia all way to the Great Wall of China itself. Rather than fight, the Nationalists eventually brokered an agreement with Japan in 1933. Known as the "Tanggu Truce," this treaty forced the Chinese Nationalists to cede territory one hundred miles south of the Great Wall as a special demilitarized zone.

The agreement also forced the Nationalists to officially recognize the Manchurian puppet state of Manchukuo as an independent country. As bad as these measures were, however, it managed to win the Nationalists a short peace with the Japanese so that they could once again turn their guns back on the communists.

It was this renewed attack against the communists that led the forces of Mao Zedong to begin the trek that came to be known as the "Long March." The Long March was actually an extremely long, protracted retreat that Mao's Red Army began to undertake from October of 1934 to October 1935 as they fled the resurgent advance of the Nationalist Kuomintang Army.

It was during the course of this march that Mao began to really come into his own as an officially recognized leader of China's communist party. As the remnants of the Red Army made their retreat west and eventually north, it was under Mao Zedong's initiative that the communist army abandoned its heavy artillery in favor of traveling light and resorted to guerrilla warfare tactics rather than facing their enemies outright.

Under Mao's direction, the Red Army was able to evade a much superior force by being erratic, starting and stopping several times and engaging in marches and counter-marches that left the enemy confused and unable to follow. In the middle of this Long March, Mao's forces also managed to capture a few cities such as Zunyi. It was here at Zunyi that Mao's communists were able to hold a special conference that would forever decide the fate of the Chinese Communist Party.

It was here that Mao was elected as chairman of the politburo, and due to strong support Mao had garnered from the leader of Soviet Russia, Josef Stalin, Mao was able to rise to the top of party leadership as well. In November 1935 Mao was officially put in place as the chairman of the Military Commission of the CCP, making him essentially the de facto leader of the Chinese Communist Party, even though it wouldn't be until several years later in 1943 that Mao would be named the official chairman.

Mao's long march ended when he arrived in the Shaanxi province here he was able to meet up with the already established communist base in the area and reorganize the 20,000 some troops that had managed to survive with him during the journey. After a year of consolidating his base, Mao set up a new headquarters for the CCP in the nearby crossroads town of Yanan. This move would prove to be an even greater crossroads in Mao Zedong's own personal life.

During a bombing raid, his wife He Zizhen was nearly killed when shrapnel tore through her body. Shortly after this trauma, He Zizhen, who had been pregnant for most of the Long March, gave birth to a baby girl, who was then delivered to a local peasant family for safe keeping. He Zizhen was then rushed off to Moscow to receive emergency medical treatment for her wounds.

Rather than being a supportive husband, Mao took He Zizhen's sick leave as an opportunity to divorce her and become involved with a famous Chinese actress named Jiang Qing. Mao would eventually marry Jiang Qing, despite opposition from other party members, on November 28th, 1938.

Hi Zhizen would never quite recover from the trauma of her injuries and her divorce from Mao, and after being treated in Moscow, she suffered a series of mental breakdowns before being transferred to a mental institution in Shanghai, China.

With his new personal life established, Mao set up solidifying his political standing. The first step would be creating his own truce with Chiang Kai-shek so that he could turn all of his energy on the Japanese. On May 5th, Mao telegrammed the Military Council of the Nanking National Government to propose an alliance. Complicating this olive branch, however, was the fact that Chiang Kai-shek was determined to refuse such overtures and continue the conflict against the communists.

In regard to why he would rather focus on cracking down on Chinese communists than the aggressive incursions made by the Japanese, Chiang Kai-shek stated, "the Japanese constituted a disease of the limbs, but the communist affliction lay close to China's heart." This sentiment perfectly exemplified the hardline Nationalist policy of "internal consolidation first, expulsion of foreign encroachment later."

The only thing that forced the nationalist leader to come to terms with Mao finally was the infamous "Xi'an Incident." It was in the provincial city of Xi'an in Northern China when Chiang Kai-shek sent one of his generals, a former Manchurian warlord named Zhang Xueliang, to engage local communists in a battle that things took a decided change of course.

Upon arriving at Xi'an, rather than fight the communists, Zhang was so impressed by their organization and command structure that he wished to recruit them for what he viewed as the "bigger fight" against the Japanese. Once Chiang received word of this, he was, of course, completely infuriated, and immediately flew out to Xi'an himself to deal with what he viewed to be nothing more than blatant insubordination.

Rather than being able to coerce General Zhang into listening to his demands, Chiang Kai-shek was immediately arrested by Zhang's personal guard and incarcerated until on Christmas day, December 25th, 1936 he finally assented to forge an alliance with Mao and the communists against the Japanese. This was a great Christmas gift for many in China who were suffering under the strain of Japanese oppression and longed for some form of Chinese unity and solidarity against the threat.

This gift of a tenuous unity came just in time to meet the Japanese threat of full-scale invasion, as the Japanese war machine broke out of Manchuria and mercilessly attacked the cities of Shanghai and Nanking. Sparking one of the most brutal and infamous incidents of World War Two, China launched into a full-blown apocalyptic showdown with the Axis war machine of fascist Japan.

Chapter Five

From Nanking to Pearl Harbor

"Despise the enemy strategically, but take him seriously tactically."

—Mao Zedong

China's entry into what would become World War Two was marked by one of the worst massacres to befall any country that was pulled into the conflict. When on that rather unlucky day of December 13th, 1937, Japanese troops marched into Nanking, China and unleashed a veritable hell on Earth for its citizens.

It was under the specific orders of Japanese General Matsui Iwane that, in order to break the back of Chinese resistance, normal rules of warfare were completely disregarded. General Matsui—who after World War Two would eventually be executed for his war crimes—gave his troops implicit instructions to burn Nanking to the ground and make the civilian population pay a heavy price.

It was these orders that gave Japanese soldiers the green light to launch a campaign of unheard-of atrocities against the average Chinese citizen that would become known as the "Rape of Nanking." Sadly enough, the title of this wartime engagement is not so much allegory as it is a quite literal interpretation of events, stemming from the fact that Japanese soldiers very much did rape their way all throughout this historic former Chinese capital.

In the course of the onslaught, tens of thousands of Chinese women and even young girls were systematically ripped from their homes and brutally subjected to gang rapes by Japanese soldiers. Some of these women were quite literally raped to death, dying from the repeated sexual assaults that were inflicted upon them. While for the most part Chinese men were spared the horror of sexual assault upon their own person, they were quite often made to watch the denigration of their own wives and daughters before they were executed themselves.

For the Chinese soldiers who became prisoners of war, an even worse fate than death often awaited them as the Bushido Samurai culture of Japan had no respect for those who surrender. Any POW's under their charge were left to languish in unspeakable conditions and were systematically tortured until they breathed their last breath. 150,000 were exterminated outright.

After the Rape of Nanking finally concluded itself, this once majestic Chinese city, plundered and looted of all its resources, had been left a smoking ruin with a traumatized Chinese citizenry buried in the ashes of Japanese conquest. While the Nationalists were suffering heavy losses in Nanking, Mao was reorganizing his own troops; by August 1938 his Red Army had formed special battalions known as the "Eighth Route Army" and the "New Fourth Army."

These units were readily mobilized and sent to the battlefront to join KMT forces as early as January 1938. However, Mao and his Red Army wouldn't have their first major military victory against the Japanese until August of 1940 during the "Hundred Regiments Campaign." By 1940 the Eighth Route Army led by Zhu de had swelled its ranks to over 400,000 men.

This fighting force would go on to attack railway lines and other sites of strategic importance to the Japanese between August 20th and September 10th 1940. During these attacks, council's tunnels, bridges, and railway stations vital to the Japanese war effort were destroyed. Immediately following the destruction of this important infrastructure, the Chinese communists went on to attack the Japanese bases directly.

The Japanese initially suffered heavy losses, with over 12,000 regular Japanese soldiers and over 5000 troops from the puppet state of Manchukuo (Manchuria) being killed. It would take the Japanese several months to recuperate from this important and devastating offensive launched by the communists.

The success of Mao's guerrilla fighters was more of a propaganda boon than anything else, greatly bolstering his popularity with the average Chinese citizen, making the communists seem much more successful than the wavering forces of Chang Kai-shek. The Nationalists of Generalissimo Chain Kai-shek were about to receive a great boost, however, in the form of another aggressive move from Japan - the 1941 bombing of Pearl Harbor.

Chapter Six

Consolidating Power

"All reactionaries are paper tigers."

—Mao Zedong

Even though most Americans were completely surprised by the Japanese attack on Hawaii that occurred on December 7th, 1941, the Pentagon in the United States was well aware of the possibility. Tensions between the United States and Japan began in earnest when Japanese forces invaded the French colony of Indochina.

The colony of Indochina was a conglomeration of modern day Laos, Cambodia, Vietnam, Thailand, Myanmar, and parts of Malaysia. The invasion occurred shortly after France's capitulation to Nazi Germany, in one of the more stunning upsets of World War Two.

The motives behind such an invasion were purely material. Japan had been struggling for resources, primarily oil, ever since the start of its aggressive campaigns of expansion, and French Indochina was a promising place to begin procuring fuel for the Japanese Empire. Japan also sought control of this bit of colonial real estate in order to prevent the flow of supplies from the French colony, on over to China.

The United States, which was financially supporting both China and the French underground's resistance to fascist oppression, did not take too kindly to these latest developments of Japanese aggression, to say the least. In order to make their displeasure known, immediately after this attack, all U.S. shipments of aviation fuel and other equipment to Japan were ceased.

Many in the United States government saw the Japanese attacks on these French overseas possessions as a prelude to even more aggressive actions in the future that would cause the Imperial Japanese army to collide with U.S. interests in the Pacific. These first initial U.S. sanctions against Japan were then followed up by an all-out oil embargo against Japan in July of 1941.

This move then led the oil-starved Japanese war machine to deliver one last offer to the United States on November 20th, 1941, offering to remove all troops from Indochina if the sanctions were lifted. The United States were firm, however, and demanded that Japan not only evacuate the French Colony but remove all of its troops stationed in China as well.

The policy makers in Japan felt that withdrawing from China would be an unthinkable loss of face, and so the plan to attack the U.S. naval fleet in Pearl Harbor was launched. However, if Mao Zedong thought that he had gained an ally in the struggle against Japanese imperialism, he would have to think again.

As United States efforts to aid China went from underground aid to outright, direct military and financial support, Chaing Kai-shek became their go-to guy, and the Generalissimo made it clear that he would not tolerate any aid to the communists. As a result of this insistence, virtually no aid was given to Mao Zedong and his guerrilla fighters during the entire course of World War Two.

While the nationalists were being served up new U.S. made warplanes, machine guns, and even uniforms; the communists had to make do with whatever leftover equipment they could scrounge together, often resorting to picking up weapons and artillery pieces that were left behind by the fighting Japanese and the Chinese

Nationalists. Becoming the dumpster diver of the battlefield, Mao's communists mostly stayed holed up in the safety of their Yanan stronghold in hard-to-reach North Western China and avoided combat for much of the rest of World War Two.

Mostly left undisturbed while Chain Kai-shek's forces duked it out with the Japanese, Mao turned his focus inward and engaged in what would be known as his first "thought reform campaign." Long before the Cultural Revolution would take shape, Mao from his base in Yanan began what would be known as the "Yanan Rectification Movement" in which the communists sought to "rectify" any wayward ideologies that they felt did not align with the official party line.

Another thing that Mao, in particular, was seeking to rectify was unwanted influence from the Soviet Union. Mao, although an admirer of Soviet Russia, did not believe that the same formula used by the Soviet Marxists would work in China, and sought to cleanse the Chinese communists of ideology that seemed "too Russian" based in its makeup.

During this period, Mao would actively isolate any wayward ideologues and force them into "study groups" that were meant to rectify their thoughts. By the time that Mao's rectification campaign came to a close in 1942, he had managed to forge a party platform for the CCP that was vastly different from the top-down, centralized command structure of the Soviet Union.

In the formula that Mao developed for the Chinese communist, a special emphasis was made for a decentralized rule that gave much autonomy to local leadership. There was also much more of an effort to develop a close relationship in the local population, stressing that all communist officials should live a simple, more egalitarian life with their environment.

Much of this sentiment was derived from Mao's own simple upbringing in the countryside, giving him a strong pull toward adopting more rustic and Spartan lifestyles for party members. After the dropping of two nuclear bombs on Japan in 1945 ended World War Two, it would be Mao's newly reformed communists that would take the struggle of their newfound ideology straight to Chaing Kai-shek and the Kuomintang.

Chapter Seven

Spending His Political Capital

"From the barrel of the gun grows political power."

—Mao Zedong

Immediately after the end of World War Two in 1945, the communist party of China held a referendum in which 1.2 million communists attended, and Mao Zedong was elected official Chairman of the CCP. After this official coronation, Mao's top lieutenants became fellow Long March veterans Zhou Enlai and Liu Shaoqi. It was Liu who would write the new constitution of the Chinese communist party.

Shortly after this final consolidation of Mao's CCP, the Kuomintang Nationalists, who had just seen the successful defeat and withdrawal of Japanese troops, invited Mao Zedong to meet with Chiang Kai-shek at his base in Chongqing, Sichuan.

This meeting was a highly publicized event with many international journalists covering the encounter. Mao proved himself to be quite an actor for the occasion and was seen giving toasts to Chiang Kai-shek's health and promising to work with Chiang toward a unified agreement for China.

However, shortly after this display of cordiality, Mao privately commented to his associates, "Chiang Kai-shek has lost his soul, he is merely a corpse and no one believes in him anymore." Mao Zedong apparently didn't believe in the peace agreements he signed with Chiang during their meeting in Chongqing; just a couple of months later the two rival armies were fighting over the power vacuum that the Japanese had left behind in Manchuria.

In the last few weeks of World War Two, the Soviet Union had launched its "Manchurian Strategic Offensive Operation" in which the Russians cleaned out the remaining Japanese troops and inserted itself as the occupying power. When the Soviets finally withdrew from Manchuria in March of 1946, they made sure that the Chinese communists moved in right behind them.

This set the stage for one of the very first proxy wars of the Cold War, with the United States backing Chiang Kai-shek and his Nationalists and the Soviets rooting for Mao and his communists. An ever pragmatic and cautious Josef Stalin advised Mao to show restraint, fearing to provoke a strong response from the U.S. These warnings from the Soviets went on deaf ears however as Mao, who had been mostly reserving the Red Army's strength during the war against Japan, unleashed its full fury upon his hated enemy Chaing Kai-shek and the Chinese Nationalists.

Like a sleeping dragon, the sheer ferocity and dedication of Mao's army seemed to take the Nationalists by surprise; once stirred to action, they managed to beat the better-equipped Nationalists in engagement after engagement until Mao's troops were successfully marching through Beijing in January of 1949. By September the war between the Nationalists and the Communists was all but over, and Chiang Kai-shek and what was left of his army fled to the island of Taiwan.

There he founded what would remain the unofficial government of the "Republic of China," where an uneasy standoff exists to this very day just off the shores of the mainland. Meanwhile, Mao declared his possession of the mainland as the *"People's Republic of China"* on October 1st, 1949.

After decades of hiding in the mountains and living like a vagabond, Mao Zedong was now the undisputed leader of the most populous country on the planet. Even for a communist, Mao now had some major political capital, and he fully intended to spend it.

Chapter Eight

Mao's Stranglehold

"The Chinese People have stood up."

—Mao Zedong

Shortly after consolidating his power in the newly proclaimed communist state of the People's Republic of China, Mao Zedong made his first official diplomatic trip abroad, heading to Moscow to meet up with the leader of the Soviet Union, Josef Stalin. The results and reception that Mao received in Russia were mixed at best. Mao was able to secure a large sum of aid from the Soviets, scoring the equivalent of about 300 million dollars' worth of financial support.

To Mao's dismay, this aid came at a price; Mao was forced to cede Chinese territory in Mongolia, allowing it to become an independent nation under Soviet protection. Mao rightfully suspected that Stalin was carving up Mongolia in order to create a buffer zone between the Soviet Union and China just in case relations go sour.

From the beginning Stalin ever the pragmatist, was not allowing himself to put too much faith in his newly elected communist colleague just south of his borders. Mao left his talks in Moscow feeling snubbed, belittled, and distrusted, but he didn't have long to belabor on these obvious deficiencies that he had with his Soviet counterpart because more pressing matters soon came to the forefront in June of 1950 when war broke out on the Korean peninsula.

Following Japanese defeat in 1945, Korea was split along the 38th parallel between the United States and the Soviet Union, creating two separate spheres of government - a communist north and capitalist south. It wasn't long before the communist north was sending troops to take over the south with the full support of the Soviet Union and China.

A United Nations force, led by the U.S., were initially successful in driving back the communist North Koreans, forcing them all the way back to the Chinese border. It was at this point that Mao made China an official participant of the conflict in October of 1950 and sent Chinese troops across the Korean border to enter the conflict. Fighting was then pushed back to the 38th parallel where the battle raged for nearly 2 more years before an armistice was signed on July 27th, 1953, creating the Korean Demilitarized Zone that has separated North and South Korea ever since.

Tens of thousands of people were killed during the Korean War, including Mao Zedong's own son Anying, and in the end, after all of the bloodshed, nothing could be said to have been accomplished, and nothing changed. This is the supreme irony and tragedy of the Korean War; at the beginning of the conflict Korea was split in half at the 38th parallel, and then after 3 years of bitter back and forth fighting, Korea was still split at the 38th parallel, exactly where it started. Neither side seemed to gain anything except thousands of dead soldiers.

Even so, Mao Zedong viewed the conflict as a win for China, since the communists managed to stand up to the United States and lived to tell the tale. Korea also proved to be a good distraction for Mao, since while U.S. troops were bogged down on the Korean peninsula, Mao Zedong took the opportunity to send the Red Army southwest in an invasion of Tibet, crushing the Tibetan independence movement and formally annexing the region to China.

Most of the world focused on the raging conflict in Korea, turning a complete blind eye to Mao's conquest of Tibet. In an after-the-fact explanation for the forceful merger, Mao Zedong simply stated that the seizure of Tibet was simply China returning to its rightful ancient borders. After the confiscation of Tibet and the Korean crisis came to a close, the rest of 1950's communist rule under Mao Zedong would be marked by drastic changes in the status quo of Chinese society.

Mao initiated sweeping campaigns against bribery, corruption, and tax evasion, among other things, in order to eliminate the previous chaos and instability that had been created in China's fractious warlord-ruled past. Much more than this, it was a land reform that managed to turn Chinese society completely on its head. The poor were given free rein to dismantle and take over the estates of the rich.

Although Mao envisioned a future society with no land owners and everyone simply sharing large communal farms, for the peasants that were part of these land grabs, they believed that they were finally getting their fair share, and were ready to hang on to the land they stole for dear life as their little piece of the land redistribution pie. This effort of the peasants rising up and taking matters into their own hands became known as the "Settling of Accounts" movement.

This was sort of sarcastic euphemism in reference to the fact that, for many of the indebted Chinese peasants, they felt that they were forcibly settling their accounts with the rich landowners with whom they were in debt by seizing the land of the ones they were indebted to. These seizures were invariably bloody and brutal, with mobs of peasants torturing countless merchants, landlords, and nobles. Mao, for his part, never implicitly supported such violence, but he never discouraged it either and would later simply shrug it off as a necessary evil for the emergence of a truly communist state.

Often just as deadly as the battle over land, however, was the battle over ideas, and in this battle of ideology during the 1950's, just as was the case in the early 1940's during the rectification campaign, Mao's thought police were out in full force. Having set up local study groups in schools and factories in order to make sure that no one deviated from proper Maoist doctrine, all of the Chinese society soon became rife with fear of being deemed retrogressive to the cause. Soon neighbor was turning against neighbor in order to demonstrate who was the most loyal to the revolution.

As a result, of all this focus on pure ideology, millions of Chinese became incarcerated in work camps for nothing more than their perceived "bad thought" processes. This, of course, created a "Salem Witch Trial" type effect, in which, just like the innocent people that were killed in Salem, Massachusetts for no other reason than their neighbor claimed they were a witch, a similar sort of witch hunt was on the march in communist China.

Without any evidence whatsoever, one neighbor who simply disliked another neighbor could claim that the person next door was against the revolution and have the person they don't like shipped off to a prison camp. This kicked off a toxic social climate of extreme distrust whose ramifications can still be felt in Chinese society today.

It was also during this climate of Mao's thought control that Mao Zedong acted out on a long-held disdain for intellectuals. Viewing many of the Chinese intellectual elite as a pompous waste of resources, Mao began forcing academics, scholars, writers, and professors to clean toilets and do other menial tasks, simply because he felt they should "get their hands dirty."

This is the sort of lunacy that a totalitarian regime can bring about; it's just surprising at how efficiently Mao's minions carried out such bizarre directives. By the mid-1950's Chairman Mao's stranglehold on Chinese society appeared to be complete.

Chapter Nine

Mao Loses Face

"War can only be abolished through war, and in order to get rid of the gun it is necessary to take up the gun."

—Mao Zedong

After several years of ruthless totalitarian rule, in 1957 Mao would shock Chinese society once again when he appeared to go soft on his previous directive. In a new social campaign that he called "Let a Hundred Flowers Bloom," he dismantled his thought police and called for all Chinese citizens to do a sort of collective analysis of the state of their union. Shocking everyone, Mao seemed to be calling on the average Chinese citizen to voice their honest opinion of how the revolution was proceeding.

Whether this was a purposeful ruse to lure out any remaining dissenters, or if Mao truly thought everyone would praise him with his or her happy remarks remains unclear, but immediately after several clear criticisms of Mao's practices came forth, Mao called for a complete crackdown on the very people whose forthright opinions he had just encouraged.

Mao immediately stated that his "Let a Hundred Flowers Bloom" campaign was now entering a second phase in which he would "pluck the poisonous weeds" from his "fragrant flowers." As a result, anyone who had anything negative to say during Mao's request for the public's honest opinion was immediately neutralized. Divide and rule were a part of Mao's strategy, and in order to stay on top in Chinese politics, he wished to keep a safe bubble of chaos between him and any possible dissent or competition of thought.

During this period Mao would constantly change his policies, sometimes almost on a whim, and this schizophrenic style of leadership would cause all of China to suffer as a result. However, at least on an economic level, nothing could quite compare to Mao's latest whim to rapidly industrialize his nation in his pet project that became known as the "Great Leap Forward."

Beginning in 1958, Mao launched his ambitious five-year plan in order to advance and modernize China's faltering infrastructure rapidly. As this plan was initiated, the Chinese central government vigorously took control of all factories and industry in the cities and finally laid full claim to all of the lands in the rural countryside, effectively evicting the peasants from the land that they had fought and murdered the previous landlords over.

In these new government-run collectives, Mao also insisted that the average Chinese peasant was fully capable of smelting steel without any formal training. Believing that if they were simply given blast furnaces and the tools needed to make industry happen, the average Chinese citizen in the field could make all the machinery and materials they need in order to build roads, bridges, and dams all over China.

Mao believed that the reason why China was backward wasn't because of a lack of training or education; it was simply that the average Chinese worker had been denied the proper tools to do the job. So it was that in his great leap forward, he sought to compel a massive pool of inexperienced and unskilled labor to complete his ambitious industrial projects.

Mao's theory proved to be horribly lacking, however, when most of the steel that was produced by the untrained workers in the collectives were of such poor quality as to be virtually unusable. There was also widespread bridge collapses, dam failures, and the roads were barely usable, as a result of such massive unskilled labor that focused on quantity rather than quality.

As a result, by 1960 China's economic and industrial state was a complete disaster. Despite the efforts of collective farms, famine was everywhere, and no matter how many factories sprung up, due to ineffective management, China was constantly short on raw materials.

Mao's colleagues in the CCP finally had to question Mao's ability to lead the nation. As a result of his dire failures, other senior members of the party such as Liu Shaoqui and Deng Xiaoping found themselves forced to exert more control just to save the sinking ship that China had become.

Members of the CCP were not the only communists that had become disenchanted with Mao; so had the Nikita Khrushchev-led Soviet Union, which began to view Mao's maverick tendencies with deep suspicion and concern, a concern that couldn't have become any more manifest than when in 1962, right in the middle of the Cuban Missile Crisis that had pushed Khrushchev's Soviet Union and Kennedy's United States to the brink of nuclear war, Mao took the opportunity to attack India.

This was classic Mao sleight of hand strategy and very similar to how he directed the invasion of Tibet while the world was busy watching Korea. When both the Soviets and the Americans were locked into a death stare with each other over the nuclear missiles in Cuba, Mao thought it was the perfect time to send Chinese troops over the Indian border to settle a long-held border dispute in the Himalayas.

This move seemed to anger the Soviet Union more than anything else, and as soon as the Cuban Missile crisis was over and they could focus more clearly on Mao's antics, Khrushchev, defying communist convention began to support India against its own previous ally of communist China. This was the death knell in an already troubled relationship, and when the dust settled, and a ceasefire emerged between India and China, all formal relations between China and the Soviet Union had effectively ceased to exist.

Chapter Ten

The Red Guards

"To read too many books is harmful."

—Mao Zedong

By the early 1960's, Mao's communist China found itself ostracized from its big brother, the Soviet Union. Defying its former Marxist master, China decided to choose its own destiny in the annals of world communism by becoming a champion of other fledgling communist states. It became an objective of Mao to support the weaker communist regimes that were emerging in Latin America, Africa, and South East Asia.

The struggle that had emerged in Vietnam between the communist North Vietnamese and the American-backed south was of course of great interest to Mao. Just as was the case with Korea a decade previous, Mao was ready to invest finances and troops to the cause of ensuring Vietnam became a fully-fledged communist nation.

As well as bankrolling communist revolutions abroad, Mao was ready to send China itself on yet another revolutionary course as he crafted what would be known as the notorious "Cultural Revolution." The massive social campaign within China that became known as the Cultural Revolution began when Mao Zedong put his wife Jiang Qing in charge of China's "cultural affairs" in 1966.

The primary objective of this campaign was to reach out to young people and bring them back to the supposed original ideals of the revolution. Many young people became rather enthusiastic with the role that they were given, and organizing in militant bands known as the "Red Guards" they quite literally became the new generation of "thought police" who were guarding the revolutionary spirit away from what was deemed to be ideology that was deviant and dangerous to the cause.

These groups of radical young people, suddenly vested with the utmost authority direct from Chairman Mao himself, began to run rampant through schools, business fronts, and neighborhoods as they declared war on the so-called "four olds," which were, "old ideas, old culture, old customs, and old habits." These Red Guards were prepared to commit a kind of cultural genocide, destroying anything that wasn't deemed to fit into the Chinese communist paradigm, a paradigm that had been established by none other than Chairman Mao.

The young Red Guards drew their own bizarre interpretations, and these gangs of uncontrollable teenage thugs would often beat up grown men in the street for the simple offense of wearing eyeglasses. The Guards apparently deemed eyewear to be associated with "intellectual snobbery." In other words, these roving bullies thought that those who wore glasses looked like nerds and deserved a good punch or two for their deficiency in eyesight.

It sounds utterly ridiculous, and by all accounts, the Cultural Revolution was an appallingly ridiculous affair that seemed to bring out the crudest and most base and intolerant aspects of high school adolescents and used them to inflict trauma on the entire Chinese nation at large. As this abject hysteria ran its course, hundreds of thousands of Chinese were rounded up and arrested for no apparent (at least logical) reason.

After it was all said and done, hundreds of thousands more were killed in the ensuing violence. Sadly, under such intensely stressful conditions as was inflicted by the sadistic Red Guard, many were actually driven to suicide, unable to cope with the immense strain they were put under by the roving bands of adolescents constantly tormenting them.

It is said that when Mao was informed of such dire straits, he flippantly and morbidly commented, "People who try to commit suicide—don't attempt to save them! China is such a populous nation; it is not as if we cannot do without a few people." However, when actual skirmishes began to break out between the insanely zealous Red Guards and members of the actual Chinese military, even Mao Zedong had to admit that things had gone too far and began to urge the Red Guards to show some restraint.

Unfortunately, the Red Guard youth had been stirred up into such a psychopathic frenzy that even Mao's orders seemed to have fallen on deaf ears; the little monsters that he had created seemed to refuse even his directives. In the end, it took a strong show of military force to finally subdue the blood lust of the sadistic Red Guards, eventually bringing the Cultural Revolution to an end in the closing days of 1969.

Conclusion

In an incredible bit of irony, it would be just a few years after the unheard-of inhumanity and wanton bloodshed Mao had inflicted against his own people in the Cultural Revolution that Mao's government would be accepted as a full-fledged member of the U.N.; ironic, since the United Nations is supposed to be the number one world body when it comes to espousing human rights.

Although China was initially excluded from the U.N. after the 1949 communist takeover, by 1964 China was a nuclear power, as well as being the most populous country on the planet. So despite the presence of egregious human rights abuses, these two facts alone seemed to all but guarantee China a place back at the bargaining table of the United Nations Security Council, and in 1971 the United States officially withdrew its objections for Chinese membership.

These overtures were then followed up a year later in 1972 when Richard Nixon came to China for an official visit with Mao Zedong. A sitting U.S. President was then photographed smiling and shaking hands with a man who was said to be responsible for the deaths of millions. Four years later, in 1976, Mao Zedong's reign of terror would end when he passed away at the ripe old age of 82.

Even though Mao's crimes are well documented, and Mao himself often openly admitted and even bragged about many of them, over 40 years later there is still plenty of room for debate on just how this complicated figure impacted Chinese history, and world history, through his actions.

Printed in Great Britain
by Amazon

44817795R00030